OVERTHINKING

How to stop worrying, reduce stress, eliminate negative thinking and start living again

Copyright © 2020

All rights reserved. This book or any portion thereof may not be reproduced, stored in a retrieval system, or transmitted in any form, or by any means, without the prior express permission of the publisher, except for the use of brief quotations in a book review. Any person who commits any unauthorized act in relation to this publication may be liable to criminal prosecution and civil claims for damages.

TABLE OF CONTENTS

Introduction 1

CHAPTER 1: What Is Overthinking? 2

CHAPTER 2: Why Do We Overthink? 11

CHAPTER 3: Why Life is Difficult When We Overthink 25

CHAPTER 4: Pinpointing the Roots 43

CHAPTER 5: Stop Neglecting Your Mind 63

CHAPTER 6: Decluttering The Mind 81

CHAPTER 7: Holding Yourself Accountable 94

CHAPTER 8: Keep It Up 109

Conclusion 118

INTRODUCTION

Congratulations on purchasing *Overthinking,* and thank you for doing so.

The following chapters will discuss the definition of overthinking, where the modern ideas and culture around it come from, and how to turn your life around from being an obsessive overthinker.

There are plenty of books on this subject on the market, thanks again for choosing this one! Every effort was made to ensure it is full of as much useful information as possible. Please enjoy!

CHAPTER 1:

WHAT IS OVERTHINKING?

In the modern world, it's excessively easy for us to get our heads too wrapped up in our own drama and the unnecessary parts of our lives. Whether or not the project at work is going the way we want them to, how our plants at home are doing, obsessing over whether or not your friend got your text—these things take up the space of our mind every day, but we can never seem to find son to stop it. Too often, we accept these concerns as a token of a busy life and a sign of healthy productivity. These thoughts are overthinking, even when they aren't plainly obsessive. The recurring thoughts we have are also very damaging—most people that experience these kinds of thoughts often will experience emotional and mental damage somewhere down the line later in life. This book is for people who overthink and would like to understand how hurtful that can be and how their bad habits can affect them, as well as how to go about trying to stop this habit from taking over their life anymore.

First, we must ask, what is overthinking, and how is it classified? Generally, in the realm of mental disorders and psychological symptoms, a certain symptom or phenomenon becomes disorderly when it's been experienced for more than 6 months and is experienced 5-7 times a week. As for overthinking, the sensation is usually experienced much more often than this in a day, let alone a week. Just having a worrisome passing thought doesn't mean that you're overthinking or that you have a problem—everyone has moments of anxiety and concern, and to never have any anxious thoughts is even more worrisome than having them too much. However, overthinking becomes a problem when the person can't seem to get work done when they start to overthink; it affects their daily lives and stops them from enjoying the company of friends or hobbies that they might have used to love. This kind of overthinking often spirals from one thought to the next, often more extreme thought, until the person having the train of thought has reached a destination that usually ends in something intensely dramatic or upsetting.

This end result is usually effectively out of the realm of possibility as it pertains to the starting thought or problem. However, "what if?" is one of the core beliefs of someone who overthinks constantly. While most overthinkers understand that the worst-case scenarios they come up with are close to impossible, they can't help but consider the mere possibility that it will come true. It's with this point that we refer to Murphy's Law—in short, anything that could possibly go wrong during any plan will always go wrong. Although it's simply a theoretical law, which should serve as a lesson to always be cautious and prepare yourself for the worst, those who tend to overthink their situation take Murphy's Law at face value and always find themselves doting on the possibilities. The truth is that, although you should always prepare for the worst to occur in life, those things are much more likely to occur when you think negatively and assume that everything will go wrong. Whether or not you believe that we manifest in our lives what we think and feel, those who have a negative or stressful outlook are not more adapted to that mindset and therefore able to take stress more easily—on the contrary, people who are negative and stressed out about their lives are more likely to suffer from emotional breakdowns and find it much harder to deal with even mildly stressful things that wouldn't faze someone calm and relaxed, someone, who doesn't overthink.

As an anxious person overthinks more and more, their mental health at large begins to decline. Anxiety is not treated by exposure—if you try to fix anxious tendencies by exposing yourself to anxiety-inducing experiences, you will only make all your problems worse. The reason for this lies in the mindset of the overthinker—although they're trying to improve themselves by forcing themselves into stress to become mentally stronger, nothing about them has changed internally. Ideally, the person suffering from anxiety or stress would find the root of that stress, deal with it in whatever way they see fit, and come back to the stress-inducing experience with a new mindset. This way, they can overcome that stress with a fresh perspective and a new outlook on their own stress and anxiety. Someone who doesn't change their mindset will also not change from that exposure. The power we have over our overthinking is equal to the power that we develop over ourselves and the power we have to manipulate and change our mindset.

Changing our mindset from being stagnant to being open to growth is the ideal way that you can overcome any stress. It's in this way that overthinking should always be perceived as a simple obstacle in your life, instead of letting it consume you and become a part of your identity. When we let negative influences consume us, they become even more dangerous and can drive even wider rifts between us and the happy life that we wish we could possess.

Most of the power that we hold over our minds can be conjured up when we take note of our overthinking. Some signs that you might be someone who overthinks to an unhealthy degree include:

- Going from one negative thought to a different, more extreme thought for a sometimes long, drawn-out spiral of negative thinking until you've landed in a desperate, disturbing, thought, or realization. This might be triggered by anything from work, relationships, platonic or otherwise, or just the stresses of everyday life. You have a starting thought—let it be "this is difficult for me". That thought can become a thought like "everything seems difficult for me", then "why is everything difficult?", then "I must not be very good at anything if I can't succeed at anything". Finally, you arrive at the thought of utter worthlessness, "I'm not good enough for anything good." This kind of attitude only makes it harder for you to get real work done and easier for you to feel worse and worse about yourself. When you spiral, you only add on to the problem. If you have this kind of thinking, where you get on a trail from one negative thought to the next, and it feels like you don't have any control over your own thoughts, you might be an overthinker.

- You tend to lash out at other people when you're going down a negative spiral. When you spiral into negative thinking patterns, you have more of a tendency to overload yourself with those negative emotions--often to the extent where you can't keep those emotions to yourself. When these emotions bubble over, we take them out on other people to express our distress at our own feelings. For example, if we feel overly stressed at something, or we're suffering from some other intense emotion, we might feel the urge to lash out or take it out on the rest of the world—this might include someone we care about or someone who just wants to help us. We lash out at others because we lose the ability to facilitate our own feelings. When we think so much that we lose the ability to rationalize our thoughts and feelings separately, we run the risk of damaging other people. This hurts most of our relationships if we let the problems progress and become even worse.

- You suffer from chronically low self-esteem or have intense problems regulating your confidence when you need it most. When you spiral and overthink things, you put yourself in a headspace that is used to being put down or having a lot of self-hatred. When you get used to that place in your mind, you become more accepting of your own self-esteem and confidence issues, making them worse. Negative things that you think in passing become stronger and stronger suggestions which plague you for longer periods of time. When you become more exposed to these long stretches of very negative thinking, it's much easier for you to just shut down and close yourself off from the world so that you don't have to experience those emotions in such an intense fashion. This is a relatively normal coping mechanism for people who suffer from stress, but it can quickly become hurtful to the person who uses it. If you're someone who thinks they may be more prone to shutting down or shutting off from the world because you simply feel overloaded by your own feelings, there's a good chance that you're an overthinker.

- You often experience chills, shivers, or physical signs of anxiety/fatigue. Even though overthinking is almost always treated exclusively as an issue of the mind, it's also very much an issue of the body. When you overthink and stress yourself out to a certain degree, your body also becomes affected in the same way that your mind is. You may be extremely stressed over the thought of a project going wrong or a date not panning out—this stress is somewhat normal, but you might be thinking about it so often and so negatively that you begin to wake up in a cold sweat at the thought of it. You might feel exhausted when you think about it, and you might experience shivers, chills, or even aches when you think about it for too long. Letting your mind dwell on something intensely negative can take a serious toll on your body—often people who overthink don't tend to listen to the signs their brain tries to give them to relax, so they're forced to listen to their body. Not everyone with an overthinking problem experiences physical symptoms, but many do when they just can't stop themselves from spiraling.

These things are normal for someone who has a lot of trouble with overthinking and managing their emotions. However, that doesn't mean that it should be taken for granted or treated as a small or acceptable state of the body and mind. Even when you overthink, your body has a reaction to that negative stimuli, although the stimuli are self-inflicted. Even though there are a diverse number of reasons that we overthink or that people develop serious conditions associated with overthinking, they all tend to stem from similar places mentally, and within the scheme of the society of the modern, urban world. The next chapter will cover many of the reasons that these bad mental habits can develop, why they develop so fervently now as opposed to generations before, and how the issues can go unchecked for so long.

CHAPTER 2:

WHY DO WE OVERTHINK?

There are many reasons that people overthink on a daily level—everyone does it from time to time. As we move into a busier, more and more modern era, more people find their schedules cluttered and overwhelming. Everyone has so much to do and so much to see that they often forget to stop and enjoy the human experience on its own. When we're overloaded with these thoughts and the schedules of our busy lives, we begin to overthink, overloading our brains with stimuli that can riddle us with many other issues if the beginnings don't go unchecked. If someone begins to overthink every day, and they spiral out of control when they get into the habit of negative thinking this way, it can begin to seriously affect the way they live their lives. Their work and productivity go down, and their life can become less fulfilling—the stress of all their thoughts distracts from things they would normally find a lot of joy or relaxation in.

When we can't relax and enjoy ourselves, it becomes easier for us to keep piling on the stress instead of letting ourselves and our bodies recuperate. Where we might have, at one time, given ourselves a break or vacation from the stress so that we could rest and get ourselves back in mental order, this might not work if we're constantly thinking about the worst possible scenarios. In addition to this way of thinking, not letting us relax and separate ourselves from the stresses of our lives, it also normalizes a miserable way of thinking—those who overthink tend to have such stress in their thoughts because they assume that the worst will always come. Being so pessimistic about everything begins to weight down on anybody after a while. It can be exhausting with every thought you have if those thoughts are constantly about what could go wrong or fail next. Thinking about when the end of the world might be, or how wrong your day could go throughout the day will just make that negative outcome more likely. When we assume the worse, we put less effort and less energy into our work and our lives. When we don't put in as much effort as we might otherwise, the outcome is more negative than it might be if we were optimistic and more motivated to do our best every day. When we're convinced that the worst will always occur no matter how much effort we put into our lives, the negative outcome seems like a confirmation of that thought. However, the reality is that the output is directly impacted by the input—if we try hard at something and go into a project or commitment with hopes for the best which we work hard to achieve, the output of that commitment will be better because of the extra effort we put into it.

The way the modern world is structured is, in many ways, one of the main reasons, so many people have such a problem getting a handle on their thoughts and feelings—the reason that people spiral out of control and often lack the presence of mind to actively control their thoughts is mainly the way that the world around them has evolved and changed to be more demanding and more intimidating than ever. As the world progresses an all fields of work become more specialized, the people who do those jobs must become more talented, more skilled, more hardworking—otherwise, they may run the risk of having their position taken over by someone else or even being automated entirely. In this position, a lot of stress is placed on the individual in question to always be working harder. Yet, the method through which they are supposed to always be improving for this purpose isn't always clear. Often there are workers who have to improve but have no clear path through which they can sharpen their skills or develop new ones. In this case, the stress builds up even more and leads to an unhappy work life.

In the realm of social and personal life, the situation isn't much better for people who are living busy, urban lives. Socializing is becoming more streamlined and more fast-paced than ever, but social media promotes the spreading of information and makes it much easier for a person's confidence to be shattered anonymously by someone with no vendetta other than to bring down the self-esteem of others. When you go onto social media, no matter what platform you choose, you put yourself out there for potentially millions of users to see every day. Through this pipeline of information and contact, people spread a version of themselves which is idealized. Users post pictures that capture a small fraction of their lives which is romanticized to look better than it could possibly be. Whether this is to make other people envious of what looks like a perfect life, or just to make the person posting feel better about their life, it raises the bar for what is and is not acceptable to post in regards to your life. It also raises the bar enormously in regards to your personal life and how happy you should be within it. When we constantly see a version of our loved ones and strangers online which is a glamourized version of their real lives, we can feel discouraged from our dreams and goals—we see everyone else achieving their own goals as if they were nothing, and we feel inferior in our struggles in everyday life. When we feel discouraged from those goals, we're more likely to give up on them, and we fall into another spiral of overthinking. Plus, during this spiral, we also have to look at versions of other people who always look their fittest, most beautiful, and their happiest. We see other people who seem like everything in life comes easy to them, who blow through their own life and only post the positive aspects of their life and image. These images can affect the people who view them negatively—they feel as though their own lives are failing when they see other people who seem to only be succeeding. Although we're increasingly connected in the modern world, there's also a rift between the self that we put onto social media and the self that we wake up within the morning—a rift that only gets bigger with time. While we're all more connected with each other than ever before as science and technology become more and more available to the common person, we also drift further and further apart as the expectations of people on social media platforms and more generally online skyrocket.

Though the presence of online pressure can stimulate a lot of stress in your life, there are certainly other factors. Many people who have a problem with chronically overthinking tend to derive a lot of that stress and anxiety from childhood—there are many ways that the stresses which we developed as young children never truly leave us, even in adulthood. Because the mind of the child is malleable and able to be changed and manipulated easily, it's very easy for ideas to stick in our heads while we grow up, which manifests as a large source of stress if it remains unresolved. For example, consider a person who grew up with very strict parents or caretakers—they developed an intense fear of that authority because they want to do well and make their caretakers proud of them. When you're only a child, the only thing that stays with you and impacts your life is that fear of authority. Regardless of the reason, you have that fear and it sticks with you, often into adulthood. When that child grows up into an adult, they're likely to suffer from a lot of stress and anxiety because they fear the authority around them. Although they're more than able to respect that authority and be productive on behalf of it, they still feel much of that stress because they never learned how to allocate that fear of authority properly. That fear can manifest itself as a fear of your boss, still being afraid of your caregivers or parents even as an adult, or having anxiety at the thought of having to negotiate or disagree with someone you look up to. At this point, fear has become an issue that controls a large part of the person's life—their ability to function in society begins to break down because they're blocked by a social barrier that was founded when they were a child. Many people experience the inverse of this phenomenon, and they tend to be overly lax when it comes to authority figures—this derives from growing up in a home that might not have been big on consequences or punishment. Regardless of the parenting style, there will always be certain thoughts and behaviors that the authority figure leaves with the child. Those habits and behaviors develop as they get older, and they stay at the forefront of the conscious mind—the habits and behaviors become a part of the individual's personality. The personality grows and changes over time, but ultimately holds tight to the core values which were placed in them when they were younger. As they grow older, the values from the parents or caregiver become very apparent parts of the personality and the person as a whole—and often, they move on with their lives without ever needing to assess those habits and behaviors they picked up. More often than not, there's nothing wrong with their mental or emotional health which would suggest that they need to evaluate why they are the person they are and how they can make changes in regards to the behaviors they learned as children. Many people, however, don't have the luxury of walking through their life without a hitch in their emotional journey that has something to do with the way they were raised or the things which were instilled in them by their environment in youth. According to Freudian psychology, most all of the issues we develop in our lives can be traced back to the root within our childhood and our home life during that time, the way our family treated us, and the way they treated each other. Because children are so absorbent of experiences and sensations, it can be very difficult to get rid of those habits and potentially volatile behavior. Although it can be a difficult, arduous, and drawn-out process to try and reverse the effects of our childhood, it isn't impossible—and it can do us a world of good when it comes to the stress that we face now as adults.

If your stress isn't caused by a fear developed when you were a child, it may be a traumatic event experienced later in life, or an untreated illness. Or, it could just be the routine that you're in at the moment. Often, mental illness tends to go untreated unless the victim of the illness is actively aware of their condition and can reach out to professionals for help. This is often the case with anxiety disorders—all of which can cause difficulty in properly processing emotion. Those who suffer from clinical anxiety don't function the same way that people without it do in regard to overthinking and perceiving possible outcomes to a situation. Those who have anxiety or panic disorders might find a task or thought that is very difficult to maintain—consider the spiral that people who overthink tend to go down when they stumble on a negative thought. The negative thought consumes them, and they find themselves unable to process the positive outcomes when all they can seem to perceive is negative. When they can't function the possible positive outcomes of a situation in the way that someone mentally healthy may be able to, they spiral more easily and can become even more anxious or depressed the farther down they spiral. This is the case for many people, as anxiety disorders are becoming more and more prevalent in the modern world. As we interact with news headlines which are more and more concerning, and we see people online living their "best life", putting pressure on us to live up to those standards, we develop a normalization of this constant anxiety that seems to plague society at large. As it becomes more and more normal and acceptable to be interacting with all these very clear causes of stress, it becomes harder to avoid them and harder to avoid the stress that naturally comes with them. In addition to this, while the sources of stress are going up all the time, the ability for people to combat that anxiety and vent it in a healthy way is not going up in proportion to the sources of it. While we're consuming more and more media, which makes us anxious and gets us thinking about the worst yet to come, we're offered less and less ways to combat that anxiety and fight our way out of it. It's in this way that people tend to be more anxious the more they interact with technology—and that those who have clinically diagnosed anxiety or panic disorders are also more likely to interact with technology more. If you're someone who overthinks on the daily or who overthinks to an extent, which plagues your daily life and makes it difficult to function, it may be that you have an undiagnosed illness or other untreated state which is drawing you toward those feelings of panic or anxiety.

Not everyone who experiences anxiety can only resolve it with medication; however—this is often an unnecessary step for people with a lot of anxiety. Before consulting medication to solve your anxiety, observe the way that you live your life every day. How happy do you feel going through your daily schedule? Does it make you anxious just to think about the stress that comes along with your busy day, your busy life? In many cases, people feel anxious and have episodes of spiraling out of control in their thinking because they fail to recognize that their surroundings are hurting them. Take note of how clean your area is and how colorful it is. These are seemingly small and menial details that add up over time if your life in that area for an extended period. The general appearance of our living space can dramatically affect the way we feel when we're in it and, therefore, has a direct impact on our quality of life. If you live in an incredibly drab, colorless, or dirty area for a lot of your time, you will probably be more drained emotionally by it. Colors promote emotions in the brain—red promotes passion, orange promotes energy, yellow promotes happiness, green promotes being refreshed, blue promotes calm, purple promotes relaxation, white promotes focus, and pink promotes love. Having pops of colors around your living space cannot only liven up your living area, but they can also prevent you from experiencing such severe anxiety. Additionally, people tend to be happier and more positive when they work in a clean, organized environment. If your home is messy or unkempt, it might be contributing to your anxiety or stress. Also, your stress might be attributed to where you live. Some people tend to prefer more quiet places to live—and would experience a lot of stress if they lived in densely populated areas. Some people are the opposite; they love to live where the action and the people are and might experience some stress from always being in the middle of nowhere and being disconnected from other people. Assess where you live and ask yourself if it's right for you. Even if you can't move for a work obligation or some other reason which prevents you from potentially relieving stress this way, there are always ways you can spruce up your home to remind you of somewhere you would rather be. Even if you live in the city and would rather be out somewhere on a ranch, there's décor and certain color schemes that are reminiscent of this aesthetic. Use your creativity to your advantage to give your place some details which make you feel more peaceful and more at home. Even if these details are relatively minute, they can play a massive role in making you feel more comfortable in your home.

The next chapter will discuss the four main derivatives of overthinking—stress, anxiety, depression, and procrastination. All of these things are elements of a negative mental spiral. If you've been really suffering recently, it's probably due to one of these things. The key to defeating an overactive mind is not to silence your thoughts or shut down your way of communicating with other people—the goal is to allow you a calmer and more collected way to think and process emotions without becoming overwhelmed by those feelings so easily. While many people who experience overactive thinking tend to have a lot of stress in their lives already, the stress and anxiety in their lives multiply after they go down the emotional rabbit hole of overthinking. This is the self-fulfilling prophecy of the overly active mind: while you may have stress, depression, or anxiety in your life long before you begin to overthink, these problems become much worse after you develop that issue with overthinking. While it can be very difficult to beat this issue, as mental health issues tend to stick around much longer and run a higher risk of relapsing back into them, one of the most important steps to taking back your mind and your life is properly understanding what can happen to you if you don't get your brain under control. If you let your mind run wild, it cannot only control your life, but it can ruin it.

CHAPTER 3:

WHY LIFE IS DIFFICULT WHEN WE OVERTHINK

Ultimately, there are many complications which can arise when you suffer from an overly active mind—you can suffer from many different degrees of stress, panic or anxiety attacks, you may lash out at others, or even worse physical complications when you only keep piling on more and more stress. Although it can be difficult to set aside time for yourself so that you can alleviate all this stress, it's endlessly important to understand exactly what can happen to you if you don't keep yourself in check mentally—being aware of the way you can devolve emotionally is a good way to make sure you understand the gravity of your mental health, and you take as best care of yourself as possible.

Of course, the first and most obvious reason that you

should try to keep yourself away from indulging in overactive thinking is stress. Stress can come in many forms, and it can be incredibly difficult to get rid of in large amounts.

There's a certain level of stress which is completely normal and healthy to the body and mind. To this degree, it's okay to have this stress in you when you go through your daily chores. In the sense of evolution, we have evolved to always feel some level of stress so that we can better manage tasks to be more productive. When we feel a normal, healthy level of stress, we tend to be more agreeable, more alert, higher-functioning, and much greater when it comes to performance and productivity. Feeling this stress in our body is our physical and mental self's way of letting us know that we have things to do and that there's always work to be done. While it's important not to let work or productivity be the top priority in your life all the time, it's not always a bad thing to set aside time to crack down and get a lot of important work done. It can be effective in our work or school life, our social and personal life, and in our love life to have this kind of stress. The stress you feel when you're about to go out on a date motivates you to hold yourself higher and to make sure the date is a success if you can help it. Additionally, healthy stress lets us keep communication with our loved ones. It motivates us to make plans with people we care about, and it also motivates us to make good on those plans and promises. Without a little bit of stress, our life would effectively fall apart—we would almost never get any work done, we would rarely feel the motivation needed to get out of bed in the morning, we probably wouldn't keep up any of our good habits because there would be no pressure to do so. This lets our health and hygiene fall into ruin pretty quickly. Overall, this kind of healthy stress lets us live our lives in a healthy way.

Of course, there is also an unhealthy kind of stress. This happens when we let healthy stress build and build over a long period of time without doing anything to vent it or allow it to dissipate over time naturally. If we have a project, we keep putting off, the healthy stress to do work becomes unhealthy stress out of fear of failure or fear of punishment if you were to keep putting the work off. There's only one kind of stress, but whether or not it ends up being healthy or unhealthy tends to rely solely on the person experiencing the stress and how they deal with the stress on their own. Someone who is generally social and makes plans with their friends might feel the healthy stress to make the get-together a success and catch up. Someone who isn't as social or is less used to going out with other people might feel more unhealthy stress due to anxiety over the meetup. This is due to a lot of different factors—some people are just naturally less accustomed to stress and never learned how to deal with it properly, and some people are also born less able to handle stress. While part of this trait is nature, and part is nurture, the reason that healthy stress becomes unhealthy stress can also depend on the specific situation. If someone is feeling a lot of stress, neither necessarily healthy or unhealthy, they have a few choices as to how they can deal with that stress. They can either do what they're stressing out over, or relieve stress naturally through facing the point of their stress, or they can actively ignore their potentially healthy stress and let it build up into more troubling, unhealthy strain on the mind and body. When this happens, the individual is more prone to anxiety or panic attacks from that intense stress. They're more likely to have a breakdown over that stress because they haven't had the opportunity to vent it, and other complications are much more likely to arise over the failure to deal with that stress properly. In this position, the person feeling the stress has probably put off their responsibilities and has, in turn, had to deal with the extra stress of that decision. The decisions which people make every day also tend to majorly impact the kind of stress they'll have, the kind of day they will have based on the kind of stress and level of that stress, and the kind of stress they're more likely to lead if they keep making the kinds of decisions they make presently as it pertains to whether they have healthy stress, which they deal with properly and can vent if need be, or unhealthy stress which plagues them for a long time after when someone with healthy stress may have vented their stresses. The unhealthy choices made by busy people directly impacts the life they will lead.

When we develop a lot of stress in our lives, it also becomes easy for that stress to develop into something potentially more serious—anxiety. Anxiety is much less healthy than stress and can more quickly drive us to lash out at the people around us. As we grow more anxious due to experiences in the world that we have, we have a higher tendency to overthink—this forms a vicious cycle of anxiety where we overthink due to this anxiety, which only gives us more anxiety. In this way, anxiety tends to be much more chronic than stress. Stress is something that everyone experiences, no matter their walk of life. Old and young people all experience stress to some degree, and that stress has the ability to be healthy and motivating to the people who experience it. However, people who experience negative stress for a long time or to an extreme degree run the risk of developing anxiety in addition to that base stress. When someone has a surplus of negative stress which they don't act on, they get more and more used to the feeling of stress. When the feeling of negative stress becomes the new norm in our brain, and for our body, we might stop reacting as strongly to that stress—we become more used to the stress, so we become effectively numb to it. In a way, physical and mental stress is a bit like an addiction. As addiction becomes stronger, the brain must adapt and flood more and more of the addiction to the system. When we are used to large amounts of stress in our daily lives, we have to be motivated by an even larger amount so we still feel the pressure to act on the stress and get work done. In this pattern, we get more and more stress in our system until something gives or we get the work is done which is required of us. When we get too much of this stress in our body and don't act on it, we develop anxiety, which for this purpose, can be considered a more extreme version of that unhealthy stress. Anxiety plagues us even when we don't have any work to do—this is why anxiety can be such an extreme problem in the lives of those who suffer from anxiety, clinical or otherwise. With stress, you feel it when you have a job to do or when there's work to be done. When the stress becomes unhealthy, we begin to feel the lingering pressure even when there's no work to be done, or when the job we were feeling healthy stress to do has been completed. Even after we've done everything we can do fulfill a task that should make that stress go away, it only brings back the negative stress and allows it to transform into anxiety. This anxiety then fills up our brains and makes it impossible to ignore a task. In a way, some people are still motivated by their anxiety. While getting their work done or completing the task at hand can be made miserable when the stress is negative or you feel anxious even after completion, it's still a driving force to many to be productive to get their work done—even though they feel anxious regardless of whether or not their work is done, they still tend to feel some kind of relief when they've finished their work. If they know there's no logical reason for them to feel so powerless, the anxiety can feel less intense or as though it's unfounded, which can serve to calm the person experiencing that anxiety.

Anxiety can come from many different things—anxiety can develop during childhood or from behaviors we pick up when we're young, much like stress. If we live our childhood with our parents or environment placing a lot of unhealthy pressure on us about performance, tests, or doing well in school, we will likely become more afraid of taking tests and afraid of presenting our achievements to others—we fear the failure that may come with that trust we have in others. When a certain pressure is heavily placed on us in childhood, it tends to follow us up through our high school years through college, and even into our adult lives. Though perhaps we "should be" focusing on doing the best we can and making our lives good and providing for our families, there are often emotional blockages that prevent us from living the best life we can live. These blockages keep the path to the happiest version of ourselves closed off from our present selves, and they keep us away from doing what makes us the happiest. The blockages in our lives can come in many forms, and they can affect every part of our lives. The fear of failure, fear of authority, the laziness we sometimes feel when we don't feel like we can keep going through our daily routine—all these things pile up on top of us and, if they aren't vented properly, they can pose a massive issue to our mental health and the way we live our lives. One of these blockages is usually some kind of anxiety. The crushing weight on our chest that makes it feel like we can't do anything that we'll never be good enough that we'll never be special enough, and everything else we feel and think in the darkest part of our mind. The fear of inadequacy is disturbingly common in people who work busy lives, people who work with technology, or in-office jobs. Sometimes the rut we dig ourselves into compounds on us all at once, and we can't help but feel suffocated by our own choices and the circumstances we have put ourselves in. Anxiety is a beast, if only because it's so difficult to uproot from our lives, but when we can take hold of it and get a handle on it independently, we can shift our lives into a much healthier path—one which is calmer and more collected, not filled with the panic and anxiety that we might be used to.

The antithesis to anxiety, however, can be just as damaging to people's mental health as the anxiety itself. While anxiety can keep you up at night and drive you seemingly insane with thoughts about the worst to come, what people in your life think of you, how much time you have to do your work, and a million other stressful things that can plague you on the daily, it can also be very damaging to the human mind to find that you just can't will yourself out of bed, can't find the strength or the energy to care about even the most basic things in your life—this feeling of anxiety which may feel endless, can be accompanied by depression. Though depression is often described as the opposite feeling of anxiety or mania, depression is perhaps most accurately described as "the absence of emotion". If you feel as though you have no purpose in the scheme of your work or social life, you often struggle to find the willpower to go through your day or complete even relatively basic chores, or you can't often will yourself to think positively, you might be struggling with a bout of depression or a depressive episode. These depressive episodes are characterized by feelings of worthlessness and that your place in the world is ultimately irrelevant, that the world would go on well without you, or even that the people in your life would be better off if they had never met you. Depression can often accompany anxiety and stress when it comes to overthinking—when we arrive at the most negative thought on the chain of the overactive mind, it usually ends in a very anxious place, or a very depressive place—if not both.

There are many qualities that depression tends to share with anxiety, in addition to their differences. While some people pant anxiety and depression as complete opposites of each other, they both tend to be navigated and built up by a sense of fear. Going back to the root of childhood, a child who grows up with a fear of failure may feel anxiety when they think about the possibility of not meeting expectations. However, they might also feel a strong sense of depression when they consider this possibility. Though they each stem from the same fear, the negative thought manifests itself in two very separate ways. While someone more anxious might fret over the worst possible outcome of a problem, someone who tends to become more depressive when they overthink might not worry so much at the possibility of a negative outcome, because they can only perceive negative outcomes or have seemingly made peace with what they perceive to be an inescapable outcome. When you think that there's no way you can get out of a bad situation, you might just resign to the negative fate and cope with it by shutting down your emotions, shutting other people out instead of feeling your emotions and putting productive energy forth into finding a way out of that problem. A depressive episode is also often characterized by general physical fatigue in addition to the mental exhaustion felt by those who suffer from depression or depressive episodes. When we exhaust ourselves mentally, that exhaustion tends to carry over into our physical bodies. Consider sleep as a direct link—when we sleep a healthy amount, we ideally feel physically refreshed and relaxed because our body and mind have both been allowed to charge metaphorically. In the case of insomnia, the body and mind have little chance to rest, so both the mental and physical self both suffer because they haven't been allowed the time or space to charge up. When we go through a depressive episode, we don't let our minds rest because we're so focused on negative, pessimistic thoughts. We're too sucked into our own depression and self-pity to recognize anything else going on, so we keep going and going in our minds until something happens to break the cycle of depressive overthinking. Because we spend so much time in that depressed thinking pattern, we exhaust our mind by not letting it take a break from that way of thinking. Even when we don't necessarily want to be thinking that way, we feel compelled into that negative spiral because of the habits that we've been building. Regardless, the mind becomes exhausted over time because it hasn't been allowed a break from the depressive thinking. When the brain gets tired and stays tired, the body begins to be affected as well. This is why, often, when people are depressed, they feel very tired. This becomes a cycle of exhaustion quickly—we don't want to get out of bed or do productive things because we're tired. This tired feeling puts us off from indulging in variety, getting out of our comfort zone, or going outside much, so we fall much easier into a depressive episode. In that depressive episode, our mind becomes tired quickly from the negative spiral. Because of the mental toll of that negativity, we feel more physically tired, and the cycle repeats.

Depression can come from a plethora of places and can look many different ways. Not everyone who suffers from chronic depression or depressive episodes looks the same. Many people hide their depressive feelings well—others seem more anxious than depressed. Often, anxiety and depression go hand in hand because they work together to get us overthinking about the future, ourselves, the people around us, and the world at large. Although they're often seen as opposing forces, they combine to make us feel bad—worse than we would feel because of any healthy or unhealthy stress we could feel. Depression may not show itself as blatantly as anxiety often does, but this doesn't mean that depression is less serious—often, those who fall on the more depressive side of the spectrum when it comes to their negative thinking tend to be more at risk for specifically dangerous or harmful behaviors. They run the risk of ruining their careers and their personal lives because they can't find the will to get out of bed and perform their life's chores and responsibilities. This can be even dangerous than someone high-functioning with anxiety—while an anxious person might feel nauseous while performing their work, a depressed person is more likely to feel just as bad, without the motivation to get the job done to feel any better.

One of the many issues that can arise from stress, anxiety, and depression is also one of the most prevalent reasons that so many people tend to overthink—when we overthink, we spend all of our time thinking over the possible outcomes of an event and little time planning for those events. Because of this, we procrastinate, and we very rarely find the motivation to get out of our own heads and do the things we've been thinking about for days, maybe even weeks. One of the biggest issues with overthinking is that it feels as though we've done so much of the work anyway. When we spend so much of our time pouring over some of the possibilities of a decision we've already made, it can be daunting to think about acting on the decisions or the thoughts we have about them. In addition, we often psyche ourselves out of action when we think too much about the decision or our options going forward. When we dote on the decisions we've made and the troubles we're probably going to have in the future because of those decisions, it can be extremely difficult to get out of our own head and act on them. Though it's important to think through our decisions and weigh our options, there's usually a time where thinking about the decisions, things we could have done, and regrets we have about the decision, become effectively useless. At that point, we only become more stressed out the more than we think about the decision. When we feel so stressed out about our decisions and our responsibilities that we stop acting on the pressure to complete tasks, we put them off to a nonexistent "better time". We imagine that, at a later point in time, we'll have calmed down and be much more able to take care of the problems we just can't seem to deal with right now. The reality is that this "better time" never really exists on its own. The best way to deal with procrastination is just by doing the thing that we're putting off. We often feel daunted by large tasks or things we have to do that feel too great, too large, too long, too important for us to handle completely on our own. This can make us feel isolated, alone, anxious, and depressed at the thought of failing with this project or chore we have to complete. Even if the thing we have to do or see or experience isn't particularly important or stressful, poor time-management skills can also contribute to having a problem with chronic procrastination. Ultimately, it becomes more and more stressful and difficult to deal with issues, the longer we put them off. This becomes a cycle of stress where we put something off because we don't know how to function or deal with the stress of it, but the stress of the task ahead only grows faster and faster the more we put it off. Plus, the longer we put off a task, the more likely it is that more projects and chores will begin to pile up on top of the first task. We also put off these other tasks until we can finish the first one, and it becomes a giant list or a giant ball of things we need to do, things we beat ourselves up over not doing, but that we still don't do because we can't find the willpower to just do them and get them over with without thinking about it too much. Procrastination is a coping mechanism for some people who don't know how to deal with large amounts of stress or anxiety, but it's a coping mechanism that can destroy your way of life if you don't keep it under control or find ways to still keep completing important tasks in your daily life.

There are many different ways that our habits of overthinking can manifest in our lives. There are also many different ways that these unhealthy habits can ruin us and break down our daily way of life. The important thing to remember is that these negative feelings and habits are all temporary if we make the decision to put an end to them and get the help we may need if we want to be mentally stable and emotionally centered. When you feel overwhelmed by your negative emotions, it might be a good idea to take a step back from them and consider what changes you can try and make to your daily life to improve your overall experience.

The next chapter will discuss the specific reasons that people tend to overthink—they can derive from childhood, from a traumatic event, or from any other number of things. Understanding why you, in particular, have an overactive mind, can help you a lot in overcoming it and managing your overthinking into something that serves you instead of actively working against you. Although it can be difficult to think of your mind as a part of you when you experience so many strong negative emotions—instead, it often feels like your brain is someone else working to actively sabotage you—the key to overcoming negative overthinking is understanding that you have to love your brain as a part of yourself, body and spirit. Only when you join together with your brain and work together with it to be better will you see the results you may not have been seeing when you were trying to fight against your mind for dominance.

CHAPTER 4:

PINPOINTING THE ROOTS

There are many reasons that we experience stress on a daily basis—they may derive from something reasonable, like the end of a stressful period, being faced with a very important burden or responsibility, or suddenly having obligations forced on you. These are things that are normal to find a lot of stress in—they're considered objectively stressful. There are also things that are generally stressful from a more subjective point of view. Some people find that having to make a lot of phone calls and coordinate a lot of people for a get together is incredibly draining as well as stressful. Others find that kind of activity very exciting. The difference lies in the experience of the individual and the ability to find pleasure in different things. This is where people develop their own personality and become unique people—your experiences as a child and young adult shape both the positive and negative parts of your character.

However, there are some times where we feel stress and anxiety from something that normally shouldn't or wouldn't make us feel this way. Maybe a specific interaction fills us with unease at work or at home that wouldn't normally have us batting an eye. Sometimes, we develop social aversions to certain experiences and feelings—much like how some people can develop an allergy over time, our negative experiences can build up into an almost irrational fear of a certain feeling or interaction. It's very important for someone who wants to get a hold of their life and their mind and to stop overthinking so they can achieve this, to understand where their habits are coming from in a more specific way. Here are some general ways that you can try and pin down what is causing your tendency to spiral and overthink;

- Meditate on your experiences—this can be difficult for people who don't normally meditate or who don't know how, especially for people who tend to overthink. People who overthink tend to have a lot going on in their minds, so it can be much harder to quiet the mind down for the sake of understanding where your negative or obstructive feelings might be coming from. Find a comfortable position where you can be very physically and mentally relaxed without being able to fall asleep. While in this position, close your eyes and focus on your breathing. Breathing deeply sets the body and mind into a more relaxed state and allows us to be calmer and focus easier. Once in this state, let your mind try to clear out on its own. Again, this can be pretty difficult when you're someone who is almost constantly thinking about something or other, so it might take some time. Be patient with your brain—although you might have some strong words for it or feel as though it's working against you, it's trying hard to process all of your emotions and thoughts and make sense of them for you. It may take a few minutes for your thoughts to peter out and become calmer. If you feel yourself spiraling while trying to meditate, take a moment to refocus yourself on your breathing instead of your thoughts, and bring your mind back to that breathing. It may take a few times of this before your brain is finally able to be relatively calm for the sake of rest and meditation. For some people, their brains never completely quiet down. Because their brain is so incredibly active, depriving it of sight or of constant stimuli can be something of a shock to the brain. However, if you practice meditation fairly regularly, even if it isn't exactly every day, your brain will begin to familiarize itself with the sensation of being gently pulled back into focus, and relaxing itself. If you train your brain like this for a long enough time, even the most distracted and overactive brain will eventually be able to calm down and cooperate during meditation. While you meditate, think of your brain as a layered organism, or a long hallway with many doors. Think of the brain as something to be explored. You are constantly growing as a person and your subconscious is always storing new experiences that build onto your personality. So, there's always something new which you can learn about yourself if you look internally. When you're in a relaxed, meditative state, it's easy for you to analyze your brain and your emotions instead of just feeling them as they come and moving on. When you think about your overactive mind, your habits of overthinking, consider how overthinking makes you feel. Do your negative thoughts tend to make you anxious or apathetic? This can point you in the direction of anxiety or depression in regards to the root of your overthinking. To be more specific, consider whether or not there may have been an experience in childhood that made you specifically anxious or apathetic toward other people? Was there someone in your life who made you feel stressed out or anxious? If this person was close to you most of your childhood, to what degree do you think they changed you as a person while you grew up? If it wasn't a person in particular or a group of people, consider a possible event that occurred that made you look differently at yourself and the way you operate in the world. Think back to this event if you can pinpoint it—try to imagine it in as much detail as possible. The more detail you can conjure up, the better of an idea you have of the reasoning behind those bad habits. Play through the experience or experiences in your mind, even if you feel stressed out or ashamed doing so. If the experience is a lot to go through emotionally, take a break when you need to before returning to it. Although these potentially traumatic people or events in your life can be draining to think about for too long, and they can exhausting to think about if they haven't been on your mind for years or if those memories have been repressed, these experiences and people are sometimes the links that we've been looking for when it comes to trying to solve our own issues, especially with overthinking and stress at large. Although the experiences can be painful or stress-inducing to live through all over again, they play a crucial role in learning more about yourself and how your past impacts you now, and can impact your future. When you face the most painful events of your past, you can become more accustomed to the memory, empowering you to learn from those experiences and better understand them.

- Backtrack the smaller decisions you make throughout the day—think about the smallest choices you make when you're at work or school, running errands, or just doing chores around your home. The way that you place things, the way that you prioritize, organize, and the way you go about making decisions can be factors in determining where your stress might come from. For example, if you're someone who doesn't like to make any lax decisions or you love the feeling of knowing every pro and con to every choice you make, you may be a bit controlling of the situation around you. Because of this personality trait, part of your stress might be coming from your compulsive need to always be in control. It isn't necessarily a bad thing to want to be in control, but not being able to ever let go of that need can cause a lot of unnecessary stress in situations where you can't exactly know everything going on around you or be in control of the decisions. When you understand the reason that you act the way you do on a more casual, detail-specific level, you can more properly address why that might be unhealthy for you and what you can do to prevent it from taking over your life. If you're someone who enjoys that control on everything around you, or who starts to lash out if you can't have that control on your environment, it can be very unhealthy mentally when you can't cope with having to give up control to someone else. Or, if you're someone who always seems to defer to someone else before you make a decision, no matter how large or small the decision is, you might have a fear of authority—the anxiety or stress you experience is less likely to arise from needing to be in control and more likely to rise from low confidence and your dependence on authority figures. Based on this understanding of your own stress and some of the reasons that you might be experiencing it, you can address it in an effective way and begin to look through ways you can cope with your stresses in a healthier way and prevent yourself from overthinking as it connects with those anxieties. If you're someone who has an issue handing over authority or control to other people and not being able to constantly monitor what's going on around you, it might be best for you to force yourself to take small steps at a time away from the control you're clinging so tightly to. Doing this little by little can really help you to be used to allowing yourself to be independent of your responsibilities. Often, exposure therapy helps to alleviate stress in people who can't seem to let go of things. When they're forced to let go instead, they often feel panicked for a while afterward. However, as they get used to the sensation of letting go and begin to associate that with the feeling of being freer from those burdens, they begin to be more and more open to letting go and letting others take over when appropriate. If you're someone on the other side who finds themselves terrified of being criticized by an authority figure or someone you look up to, this exposure therapy would probably look much different and would serve a mildly different purpose. Because you were someone who had a lot of anxiety when it comes to the idea of having to fail in front of authority, someone who felt incredibly stress at the thought of not being able to depend on that authority figure, you're not the picture of someone emotionally stable. Being too dependent on others for validation and praise can make you into a shell of a functional person, only thriving when other people let you thrive by complimenting or praising you and your work. In that case, it's best if you're in a position where you openly fail and feel through that embarrassment until you can just get back up and try again. The way most companies are structured in the modern world, especially within S.T.E.M. fields, is that a group creates a prototype or idea, and fails. After the failure, they take the understanding of how to improve based on what went wrong and they create a new prototype or idea based on those shortcomings. These companies set employees up for success by setting them up to fail—when they're able to fail and learn from it, they reach the best solution much better than someone who was right on the first try. Because the prior group failed over and over again, they understood more about the project and how they could make it better. In addition, the first group also developed a more comfortable relationship with failure and didn't take the failure personally. Someone who gets a "correct" answer the first try, however, was never enriched by better understanding their project through failure. Because they didn't fail before they succeeded, they might not understand it much as those who had to learn from their many mistakes. Also, the second group is less likely to be able to take criticism—failure is a personal slight to them, more often than not. This is the way that newer companies and education styles are able to prepare children for the real world—failure is not permanent in the workforce, and you won't be punished for not immediately understanding a new concept. Taking the time to learn and ask questions is the way that you can perform the best. If you're someone who has a lot of stress from this issue or has an intense fear of failing in front of authority, it might be in your best interest to adopt some of this thinking and incorporate it into your healing process.

- Take some time out of your busy schedule to make a new schedule of regularly self-assessing and checking on yourself. You can either take a few minutes to separate yourself from everyone else if it's easiest for you to verbalize any particularly complex emotions, or you can give yourself alone time to journal the way that you're currently feeling and why you think you might be feeling that way. You can do this every day if you want, every week or once a month. Whichever schedule works for you most comfortable and allows you to keep consistently checking in on your mental health. Not only will this help with you being able to voice your emotions and get them out into the open, but it will also help you to be more comfortable accepting your emotions as they come to you. Many people who try to stop themselves from overthinking tend to try and stifle their own emotions—they think forcing their emotions to comply with what they want them to be will help them get more control over their mind and their emotions. The opposite usually happens when we try to force compliance from an overactive mind—the brain rebels even harder and it can be even more difficult to get our thoughts under control. Instead, it's best to accept your emotions and accept that there's nothing you can do to stop yourself from feeling that way. Accept your emotions, and let them move on past you. Once you're able to accept that you don't have to be so involved in your emotions and you don't have to have an iron grip on your feelings, you can take a proper step back and be able to look at them from a new, more analytical perspective. When you separate yourself a little from your emotions—not to the extent where you feel completely detached, but enough so that you can look at them without experiencing them all over again and preventing yourself from being objective as possible—you can understand them better, as though you were an outsider looking in at those feelings. When we take a look at our sadness and see what in the past made us sad, we can make connections between events and emotions and heal ourselves going forward from there. If we notice that we start to become sad whenever we have contact with our boss, regardless of whether or not the encounter itself is negative or positive, we can then draw the conclusion that we have a poor relationship with authority which might stem from childhood or from some other experience. This is why we journal and keep consistent track of our emotions—when we check in with ourselves and begin to use this journal as a tool to notice patterns in our emotional lives, we have the ability to act on them quicker because we've given ourselves all the information we need to act. When we understand more about the way we think and we can make more coherent connections in our everyday lives that we might not have been able to make when we're too busy caught up in our feelings as they happen to us, we can act more quickly and we have a wider understanding of how we can help ourselves instead of making guesswork of our own thought processes. Journaling helps you to understand yourself better so you can help yourself better. Of course, helping yourself might not be enough if you ultimately can't dedicate all of your time to trying to figure out the best way to heal on your own. For many people who have severe anxiety or a very intense issue with overthinking, it's best to just consult a professional or someone who has an unbiased agenda to help them in their healing.

- If you feel comfortable/feel the need to contact a specialist or professional to help you with your overactive mind. While it may feel empowering to say you helped yourself before anyone else could and to insist that you know yourself better than anybody else, it's often best if you can contact someone who knows the human mind well enough so that they can help you find the best solution for you. In this case, that someone is a therapist, a psychologist, or someone else with a degree and background which gives them the understanding of the human psyche that you might not. While you do know yourself better than anyone else could, even a therapist, and it can be a large leap of faith to put your mind effectively in the hands of someone you don't know very well, therapists and psychiatrists are trained to be able to help everyone who seeks their services, and to help as many people as they can, as effectively as they can. If you're someone with an incredibly overactive mind and someone who tends to overthink, you probably have a lot of underlying stress beneath all that overthinking. Going along with this stress is probably some degree of anxiety or depression, fear, and other possibly unaddressed emotions. Just reaching out and beginning to go to therapy can be what you need to get you onto the track of healing. When you go into therapy, you meet with someone who has no agenda in your life other than to get you feeling normal again—though your friends, families, and other loved ones might have a positive agenda in your life, they still have ulterior motives and often won't make you their top priority because they also have a life and possibly a family they have to provide for. In addition, your loved ones probably don't have any kind of degree that makes them fit to take care of you as though you were their patient. They might know you well and they might be able to help you find some of the roots of your overthinking or your anxiety, but they ultimately can't medicate or prescribe anything to you—they probably aren't licensed to help you in the way that a literal professional is. Though one of the most important things to have at your disposal while you're healing is a support system of friends and your family who will support you while you recover from a destructively overactive mind, they aren't the core thing which will heal you. It's good to have friends you can rely on, but you should also have someone in your support system who has an education in providing for you medically and being able to give you the answers you need to hear and which will help you to recover the fastest. Even if you have a lot of social anxieties or you don't feel comfortable contacting a medical professional for some other reason, there are many text lines that allow you to contact trained therapists just through text who can help you in that moment. However, these text lines often don't work very well if you're looking for a therapist or someone else who will help you in the long-term to get over your unhealthy stress, overthinking, or other symptoms that might be taking a negative toll on your life. Because these therapists on text lines are temporary, it might be best to contact the text line of an actual therapist's office or just to call them. There are many professionals who will do phone conferences or similar things that allow you to get time in talking to someone who's licensed to help you without having to go into a physical office. Regardless of the way you get this help, it's very important that you have some way to contact a professional if you feel that your overthinking or your stress can't quite be totally subdued by yourself or by the other people in your support group.

It's incredibly important to have many different venues through which you can properly identify the direction your stress is coming from, the way that your overthinking is coming from. When you have a good understanding of the actual reason that you're overthinking, you're much more able to take it on, and you're able to get it under control much faster. Instead of trying many different things to get your mind under control, you have an idea of what is most likely causing your overthinking—whether it be something specific from childhood, the negative bias you might have because of past experience, or something more serious which might have gone undiagnosed or untreated. If the latter is the case, seek professional attention for whatever you may be experiencing—although it's important to understand yourself and be able to help pull yourself out of a negative spiral, it's never a good idea to try and combat negative thoughts, anxiety, or depression alone. Especially if you think you might suffer from depression, an anxiety disorder, or another medical affliction which plays a part in your overthinking, the best avenue for your mental and physical health is to seek further counsel with a professional, someone who understands you and has a degree to help you better understand what you're dealing with.

Although it's important to understand where your stress and anxiety is probably coming from, it's even more important to be able to form a plan of action as to what you'll do next to help yourself and pull yourself out of your next spiral. When you understand where your stress comes from, the actions that you take to prevent your situation from worsening become more exact, and you waste less time finding out what works for you as an individual. However, there are still a large variety of things that might or might not help relieve your stress specifically. Ideally, any form of treatment, both professional or which you can perform safely on your own, would help alleviate some stress—unfortunately, there are some methods which will help relieve a lot of stress for some, but might make that stress even worse for other people. For this reason, trial and error is important, as is taking as long as you feel necessary to figure out exactly where your stress is coming from. By self-assessing and keeping a record of your emotions, as well as considering your background and your past experiences which contribute to your personality today, you have the ability to gain more insight into yourself as a person and how you interact with the world. By observing your smaller and more minute behaviors, you might realize that some of your small habits might contribute a lot to your stress. When you see these patterns, you can understand how to change, correct, or eliminate them entirely so that you can live a calmer and happier life.

The next chapter will cover just this—ways that, based on the direction your stress, anxiety, or other negative symptoms are coming from, you can overcome your overthinking and lead a more successful life in our modern world. By adapting yourself and your habits in order to clear waste, time, and energy, you can also minimize the stress you have on your shoulders as you go about your daily life. By managing your stress more mindfully and paying attention to your body, you can achieve your highest self and, with the help of the people around you, minimize and take back control of your mind.

CHAPTER 5:

STOP NEGLECTING YOUR MIND

One of the most relevant reasons that people develop overactive minds and begin to lose track of their brain when it comes to overthinking and spiraling into a train of negative thoughts is that we neglect our minds on a daily basis. We ignore the signs that are usually very clearly given to us by our bodies and our mind. When we ignore these clear signs, the brain and body start to deteriorate because we've neglected to give them the things they need. For example, we feel hungry—this hunger is a sign that the body needs food. We feel tired when we need to rest, and thirsty when we need water or some other liquid. These are some of our body's signs that we need to provide something for it. When we don't listen to those signs, we begin to deteriorate physically as a result. Our brain behaves similarly—when it needs something or is having a negative experience, it tries to give us signals so we can fulfill it. If we don't, we begin to suffer mentally for it.

One of the greatest examples of our brain giving us very clear signals is when we go into sensory overload. Sensory overload is an experience just about everyone has at some point in their life, and it can be terrifying if you're experiencing it for the first time. Akin to a mild panic or anxiety attack, sensory overload hits us when we're having too many stimuli coming in for our brain to process and make into more consumable information; we experience a massive amount every single day, and our brain is always filing through experiences and sensations so that the conscious can experience a variety throughout the day without being fried. In this way, the brain functions much like our peripheral vision—we still see things in our periphery, but they don't take our full attention and we often don't end up focusing too hard on it. When there's just too much going on for our brain to cut down, the conscious can be overloaded by stimulus and we go into a state called sensory overload. When we go into sensory overload, we can feel panicky or extremely anxious when we hear even slight noise. We become more shaken by touch physical sensations. Our senses become heightened, but the extremity of those senses becomes unpleasant. Going into sensory overload is our brain's way of telling us that it needs to take a break from being in that environment and that it needs to be somewhere different, alone, and much calmer so that that brain can refocus. Usually, when we receive this "message", we listen because our brain is forcing us to listen, or else the discomfort worsens—we move into a different room or do whatever we can to isolate ourselves until our brain can reboot and we can take in a normal level of stimulus again. However, there are some instances where we can't leave the room or we just have to deal with the overload for a time. After a while of being overloaded, our brain can sometimes be used to it and level out again. Other times, the brain only sends more and more anxious signals to the body and the negative sensations get worse. Sensory overload is one of the most physical of the messages our brain can send us about its needs. If we don't listen to it, we run the risk of the sensory overload escalating into a full-scale panic attack.

In a way, overthinking and going down a very negative spiral of thinking is also one of our brains ways of telling us that we might want to change the environment or calm down. When we overthink, we tend to get "tunnel vision" --we stop paying attention to the rest of the world happening around us, and we only focus on those negative thoughts. It can be thought of as the inverse of sensory overload; we hone in too much on our thoughts instead of trying to focus too much on everything going on at once. It's important to learn to find that happy medium—paying attention to both other things going on around you and yourself, and your emotions so that you don't reach an emotional breaking point without even meaning to. This is the reason that people with anxiety or anxiety disorders are much more at risk for having sensory overload—not only are they more prone to suffering from an overload of stimulus, they tend to have a point which they reach sooner than other people at which they cease to emotionally function in a way that someone without any anxiety would. This is why it's so important to listen to your brain when it tries to let you know that it's being overstimulated. If you start to feel vertigo, dizzy, or overwhelmed being in a room or being in a group of people, you're probably being overstimulated and you might want to leave the group or the room for a moment so you can center your focus and come back to a "neutral" space. If you can't try to focus on your breathing or something else simple. Changing gears and focusing on your breathing not only regulates your breathing, which calms you down quicker, it also gives your brain something simple and new to focus on, which can make it less prone to being overloaded or staying overloaded. This is also how you can manage panic or anxiety attacks—change your focus to a set of smaller, simpler tasks. Think about 3 things you can see, hear, touch, etc. Being aware of all five of your main senses and using them to ground yourself can bring you back to reality and help you to stay calm in a stressful and potentially very anxiety-inducing situation. If you can't identify a few things with each of your senses, or doing so is uncomfortable or makes you anxious, try just thinking about your favorite color, what you want to do today, and what you want to see the most right now. Think about the things you enjoy the most, but keep the ideas simple and easy to digest. The answers should be things you already know very well, and simple as well as short. The more that you get used to asking yourself simple and easy to answer questions, the quicker you can bring yourself back to a "normal" level of functioning and back to a place where you can get back to whatever you were doing before your brain became overloaded.

When we get sensory overload and are forced to take a break, that short rest doesn't satisfy the brain, however. When we do this, we aren't choosing to obey our mind and give it a short rest—sensory overload is the literal breaking point for the brain in which it forces us to take a break or else we shut down. Think about the thirstiest you've ever been—when you're dehydrated, that isn't when you should drink some water and keep going about your day. When you feel thirsty, you're already becoming mildly dehydrated and should drink water more regularly. The normal body should drink water often enough and in enough of a quantity so that we never get very thirsty often. Of course, this is a sign that many people tend to neglect in their bodies because it doesn't usually show an outward appearance or sign that we're forced to notice—unless, of course, we become so dehydrated that we start to show physical signs of it or suffer physically because of it. Sensory overload behaves in a very similar way. By the time we start to get overloaded, it isn't enough to just wait until the wave passes before continuing with whatever you were doing. If you get sensory overload on a fairly regular basis, it's a sign that you should be doing more to rest your brain regularly and that whatever you're doing in large quantities that are correlating with when you have sensory overload, you need to minimize it or find a way to make it less intense or demanding on your brain. When you get sensory overload and come back down from it, it's a sign that you should not only take a quick break to rest your brain enough to keep going, but you should also take a little while when you can to rest your body and mind properly. It may be a sign that you aren't getting enough sleep, or something in your current daily routine is causing you a lot of stress, which is probably not necessary. In some cases, a lot of sensory overload on the regular might be a tell for an underlying mental illness, such as an anxiety disorder. If you find that changing your routine to be less stressful and getting a normal amount of sleep isn't doing much, or anything, to ease your stress, it might be a good idea to talk to your doctor about being put on a medication for anxiety or seeing a professional if you need help with extreme amounts of stress. However you deal with your stress, it's best to understand that but the time you experience a panic attack or sensory overload to some degree, your brain has passed the point where it's tired and needs to rest lightly. By that point, your brain is begging you to take some time away and lie down, do something gentle on the eyes and the mind, or rest in some other way that both relaxes your mind and your body. This looks different for everyone—it might be just taking a long-needed nap. For other people it might be taking a long walk out in the woods, or taking a day to catch up with friends, trying something new, or getting creative in some way that helps you relax and unwind. In addition to being a call to rest and relax, sensory overload is also a sign that our brain deeply craves something new and entertaining it can latch itself onto. The brain soaks up all information like a sponge, so it constantly needs new stimuli to always feel satisfied with itself. This is why when we take a new path to get somewhere. The ride seems shorter and shorter the more we go that direction—as we remember certain things about the path, our brain blocks out the things we already remember and know so we can more fully register and appreciate new things or things we don't remember as well. We eventually seem to block out the whole ride through that path because we know all of it and we don't need to take note of it when nothing new happens. The same thing happens with our daily routine with our lives. If nothing new happens, there's no need for us to do anything to remember it or make any special notes about it. So, the brain gets bored of this daily routine once it knows all the steps. Although some people are more accustomed to being on a tight schedule than others, and some people like it that way more than others, no one can be in the same rut forever. Having a schedule gets boring for everyone after a while, and a lack of variety can promote apathy and depression. So, in order for the brain to be entertained and to keep our spirits up, we're encouraged to try and find something new—always stepping out of our comfort zone in search of something new and fascinating. It might be a new friend, a new food, or a hobby we never thought we would love as much as we do. Regardless of the form, the variety in our life takes, we need to find that variety or else our brain becomes apathetic. As they say, "variety is the spice of life". Although variety can seem like it would be overwhelming to an anxious brain, the opposite is usually true. With the exception of people who have anxiety disorders—their brains are different from people who don't have anxiety disorders on a chemical level. They have different levels of certain neurotransmitters like dopamine, which makes them much more susceptible to become anxious very quickly—brains tend to become anxious when they have nowhere to vent their nervous energy. Because of this, the nervous energy which might otherwise be somewhat healthy, or at least constructive, gets pent up for a long enough time so that it becomes destructive and even potentially dangerous to the person. When we have no variety in our lives and nothing new that our brain can attach itself to, it has to take out that energy by making up variety on its own. This variety is often negative, feeling sudden waves of nausea or dread, anxiety, chills or shivers, feeling paranoid or nervous about a possibility, and otherwise feeling all the stress in your mind seems to manifest itself all at once. This, as you might be able to tell, is both incredibly unhelpful and unhealthy to both you and your mind, it's also very unpleasant to have to deal with. If you want to avoid this negative manifestation of stress, try to add in a more positive variety to your day.

One of the ways you can do this is by putting more intention into every decision you make throughout the day. When you make a decision, think through it longer than you might normally. Be very sure of yourself, feel yourself, and feel the confidence you have in that choice. This can ground you and also help you to generally be more confident. Put intention into waking up in the morning, be aware of yourself and your body as you get ready and dressed, brush your teeth, shower, and whatever else you do in the morning. Being mindful and in the moment not only connects you to the decisions you make, but it also lets your brain enjoy the variety of this awareness. As humans, we tend to go through our morning routine dead in the eyes—we're tired and we might be dreading the day ahead. Instead of going through our mornings with dread, it's good for our brain if we mix it up and become aware of what we're doing and why we're doing it. Instead of having what you always have for breakfast, try to have something new. It can be something healthy, something simple, something complex, vegan, anything new or different that you haven't had in a while. Get up 5 or 10 minutes earlier than you normally would. A few times a week, take this extra time before you start getting ready to do some yoga or just a few stretches. This can warm your body up and prepare you for the day. In addition, getting just a little bit of exercise in you before the day officially begins is very good for your body and mind. The morning is the best time for many people to lightly exercise—the early hours shouldn't be used for heavy exercise or intense physical activity. The morning time when you don't quite have to start getting ready yet can also be used to reflect on yourself. Think about what you have to do today in an objective way—don't think of it as a long list of things you have to do to avoid punishment. Think of it as some things you want to do so you can grow, improve, and be the best you can be. When you put intention into your thoughts and build these small habits, they set the way for you to make more, even bigger good habits to replace and kick out the old, bad habits. Just waking up a little bit earlier, going through your morning routine a bit slower, taking that extra time to stretch or just be mindful, can make a world of difference in regards to both your mind getting that much-needed variety, and also setting a positive standard for your thinking pattern. You could also use a journal that you might have been using to keep yourself in touch with your emotions to set a positive habit. In the morning, or at some point during the day, think of something genuinely positive that you thought recently. It can be something nice you noticed about someone, a certain feature of something you witnessed, or any other positive thought you had that struck you in the moment. If you don't have any that you can think of, think of anything positive that you've thought that day that comes to mind. The most positive thing you thought of should be documented, even if it wasn't something incredibly positive or a breakthrough. If you have a hard time thinking of anything very nice or positive that you thought during the day, that's a sign that maybe you should put more effort into being mindful during the day, so that you can actively look for positive things to stimulate positive thoughts and feelings, and take note of those positive thoughts for the sake of keeping a record of them. The more you get used to picking out positive feelings and thoughts, the more easily they will start to come to you on their own, and the more positive you will begin to think. And, the more you document these positive thoughts and feelings you have every day, the more positive affirmations you have to go through when you look back at all of your journal entries. Ultimately, most of the ways that you can get rid of your overthinking or minimize it begins with taking power away from your negative habits and empowering yourself with healthier, more positive habits. When you introduce your brain to more variety through positive outlets, you normalize positive thinking and positive feelings to your brain—which might be used to feeling stuck, anxious, and isolated. Introducing these positive feelings gets you back on the track to feeling like yourself, feeling happier and healthier, and ultimately being that much more in control of your body and your mind—especially your thoughts.

Something that many people struggle to understand when they first set out to heal themselves and help pull themselves out of this hole of overthinking and stress—most of the healing process can be initiated by thinking positively. Although people with actual illnesses or disorders should also seek professional help, the human mind is strong in suggestion. If we start a positive habit in our lives, as soon as we start to keep it up and it becomes integrated into our routine and into our lives, the brain adapts it rather quickly. Most brains take 2-3 weeks to truly make something into a habit that then becomes difficult to break. If you can keep a journal of positive affirmations for this length of time, or put more intention into every day for this length of time, or keep up any other positive habit that you want to adopt for this length of time, it becomes much easier to maintain the habit from that point on. The same goes for those who go and seek professional help—it takes a commitment to consistently visit a therapist or other specialist to keep consistently taking your medication if you have/need it. Additionally, most therapists will ask that you do some of these things anyway to help you to feel better without having to rely completely on them for that help.

Even something as small as going outside every day or dedicating five to ten minutes every day to meditation, yoga, stretching, or just getting up and walking around, can go a long way if you keep it up for enough of a period so that it becomes a real habit to your brain. Even though this will also eventually become a habit that your brain might get bored of after a while, there are always ways that you can change up this daily light exercise or trip outside. The point behind making these small habits is that by exposing your brain to new things and introducing it to more positive habits and feelings/thoughts, you can change the way you think rather quickly. In addition to introducing your mind and body to a more positive experience, it can also go a long way for you to just learn some basic control over your mind. This can be honed throughout the day as long as you stay aware of your mind and keep focusing on keeping your thoughts in check—however, most people find that they can help themselves the most when they dedicate regular time to meditation—sitting down on their own time and focusing in on their thoughts and on their mind. When you meditate and become aware of your thoughts, you can tell when they linger and then they start to spiral downward. When they start to spiral into something much less pleasant or they begin to give you that familiar rise of stress, anxiety, or apathy, you have more power in that moment to take control back of your mind. You shouldn't try to force your brain to stay one way or try to force it into submission—your brain doesn't obey you and you don't obey it the same. Instead, work on encouraging your thoughts in a more positive direction. When one voice in your head begins to rattle off all the terrible things that could happen today, let there be another voice which is encouraging, listing off every positive thing for the negatives. If you can reach equilibrium, you give the negative and stress-inducing part of your brain much less power. When you take that extra control away from your brain, you allow yourself the time to relax and your brain comes back to a neutral point where it's open to both positive and negative thoughts and feelings. Keep practicing this way for as long as you need to and eventually, you'll feel that your brain needs less and less encouraging in the positive direction and will simply start to shift over into that direction once you stop the flow of negative thoughts. This way, you train your brain not to fear your will or to let itself be controlled by you, but to cooperate with you and be more accepting of and open to positivity.

The way the world often bombards us with negative information, news, and fearmongering, it's easy to see why so many people just shut their brains down from the positive information that often hides behind that negative. There's a culture that exists where it's better to be negative and to be pleasantly surprised than it is to be optimistic and let down. When we do this, however, we just set ourselves up for sadness and disappointment no matter if we're right or wrong. Even if we take a negative perspective, being pleasantly surprised isn't as pleasant, as it is the opportunity for something else to go wrong. When we look at things with more hope and let ourselves feel that optimism, we open the door for positive things, even if we're proven wrong in the moment. Even if we're disappointed by an outcome, that only means that something good is more likely to come next. Basking in the positive things and accepting and moving past the negative things is the best way to live a happy and simplistic life in a world where pessimism is idolized.

The next chapter will focus on moving these ideas and some of this advice into a less professional context and into the social and personal parts of our lives. Our overthinking tends to affect our relationships more than our jobs or productivity. A bump in the road of a relationship can become rocky quickly if we don't know how to get a handle on our negative thinking and keep our mind in check.

CHAPTER 6:

DECLUTTERING THE MIND

Although the way that our mind and our thinking affect us is certainly important in the realm of work and professionalism, it's likely even more important when we retire from the workday and head home to friends and families. Our loved ones are almost as affected by our mental state as we are, so they're just as afflicted by it as us when we have a problem with stress, anxiety, depression, or anything else that goes wrong when we spiral and overthink to an unhealthy extent. When we overthink, we often become unfocused from ourselves and the people around us. When we lose sight of ourselves, our loved ones, and the way that we interact with those loved ones, we can lash out at them and hurt them without even recognizing that we're in the wrong, or realizing what we're doing to people who want to support us and help us.

One of the most important signs that you have a problem with overthinking or with stress, in general, is that you tend to lash out at other people, especially people who are close to you. People reaching out to you and trying to either be close to you or otherwise help you can be a trigger for the anger that is probably unfounded. It can be annoying if we're overthinking, in a place mentally where we struggle to keep the peace between the part of us that wants to be hopeful and the part of us which is full of anger and negative thoughts when someone randomly starts to bother us in the middle of something important. They don't seem like they understand, and it's hard to view them as a victim or someone who just wants to help us. This is because when we overthink and get into a negative spiral where we can't think straight and we don't focus on our loved ones, we become self-centered and begin to only think about how we feel and how a situation is affecting us. This happens to everyone now and then, and it usually isn't very difficult to get them back on mental track. However, for someone who's used to stress and anxiety, it can be much easier said than done. When we lash out, we only think about how annoyed we are, and we tend to perceive that annoyance as being directed at that person for bothering us or for being in our space, interrupting something or being nosy. Often, though, we're just annoyed or angry at ourselves for not being able to just make ourselves happier and more content. The annoyance we have at ourselves is interrupted when a loved one enters our space, and that annoyance gets redirected back at them even when we don't mean for it to happen that way. Because we've lost control of our thoughts, it's also easy for us to suddenly lose control of our feelings as well. We need to learn to get a grip on our thoughts and our conscious mind so that we can more easily get back in control of our emotions—the worst wake-up call for this ever is when we realize that we're hurting and damaging people who love us and who we love as well.

One of the best ways that we can really brighten up a relationship and prevent ourselves from hurting them if at all possible is to be sure to try and clear the lines of communication with the people we trust, who are close to us and who we might be hurting without knowing it. Have a miniature intervention for yourself—sit down with these people you love and tell them plainly that you're trying to improve yourself and that you know you might be hurting them or making them uncomfortable and that you haven't realized it. Ask them to be honest with you about this, whether or not you've hurt them emotionally or made them upset or uncomfortable for just trying to reach out and help you. Let the people in your life know that you're trying to make positive changes and that you want their support in it. Let them know that you care for them above all else, and you want them to keep supporting you. In addition, these people will serve as a way for you to catch yourself if you slip mentally and begin to lash out or spiral in other ways. Ask the loved ones in your life, if they're comfortable with serving as your support system while you make these important changes in your life. Ask them to let you know if they notice that you're becoming irritable or lashing out unfairly to them or to your other loved ones. Offer them ways that they can let you know they think you might be spiraling—this can be either a covert codeword or a plain and simple tug—metaphorically or otherwise—to let you know you're hurting somebody or being unfair to them. Offer them other ways that they can help you if you seem to be spiraling or having a hard time controlling your thoughts and emotions. Above all, encourage them that you care about them and that you want them to be honest and open with you so that you can be open and honest with them. Communication is always the key to any relationship and can fix just about any issue that arises within a relationship, whether it be familial, platonic, or romantic in nature. Having this communal understanding with your loved ones establishes a bond and can also help to repair a relationship that might have been damaged or weakened before you sat down to be open with them about the improvements you are looking to make to your life and your relationships. Opening these pathways of communication lets your loved ones know that you're aware of anything you've done wrong and you genuinely want to get better so that you can fix it and get back to not only making yourself feel better but also providing for your loved ones again in a healthy and happy way.

It's often a good idea to have someone who understands you not only on an emotional level but on a professional level, to be a part of your support system. Even if you don't necessarily have a diagnosed illness or an anxiety disorder, that doesn't mean that going to a therapist or some other professional in the field isn't right for you or can't help you. While it's usually good to have a support system which is mostly made up of friends and family, it's also a good idea to have at least one person who you can contact if you need to who has an unbiased opinion of you, has little to no agenda in your life, and has a background which enables them to help you in a way that the other people in your support system simply can't. Having a therapist or other specialist offer a medical opinion of what you should do while you try to recover and get better as a person trying to redirect their brain and get their emotions to a healthy place can be of massive help when you feel stuck. When you feel that you've hit a plateau on your emotional/mental recovery, it can be easy to turn to a friend and vent your frustrations. It's a good idea to do this, and it can make you feel more comfortable and less alone to have the support of someone you know who cares for you and has your best interests at heart. However, you shouldn't only turn to someone you know. In addition to having the ability to contact someone personally close to you, you should also be able to get real medical advice from someone who knows you and knows the subject matter from the perspective of someone who has made a career out of understanding subjects like anxiety and stress. While it can be more emotionally relieving to confide in a friend or family member about your frustrations, you're more likely to get an actual working solution from someone who has a degree or background in the psychological or medical field.

While you're on this path to recovery, be sure to check in regularly with the people in your support system. Not only will it be a relief to you to have this path of communication regularly open, it's also a relief to the loved ones in your support system to know that you still want to have that path open for them to be honest and upfront with you about your path to a better, happier life. While you have these check-ins, ask them things about the past few weeks or few months, or however much time has passed since you last checked up with them. Ask them how they've been feeling about you and about the progress you've made—ask if they can see a positive change and if they like the changes they see. While you shouldn't rely on them for medical diagnosis or take all their criticisms to heart, it's always a good idea to get opinions and thoughts from the loved ones who are supporting you through this. Ask them if they've been made uncomfortable or if you've lashed out at them since the last time you checked in with them. How severe was that lashing out? How irritable did you seem to be afterward? How much have you been lashing out since the last check-in, and have you gotten better or worse about lashing out at people? Although ideally, you would be the one most in control of your thoughts and your feelings, we often need other people in our lives to check up on us and make sure that we aren't hurting others or ourselves. In the process of checking in, ask about the people who are in your support system instead of only asking about yourself. Ask about how they've been and what news they have to share that they might not have told you yet. Opening communication should serve not only you on your journey, but them as well. And, letting them open up during these check-ins normalizes asking about other people and being attentive to other people's feelings. When we spiral often and we overthink often, our brain gets used to not only the stress of that but also the focus being only on ourselves and how we're suffering because of that overthinking, because of this, the brain needs to be reminded that it's good and important to focus on other people sometimes. In addition to talking a lot to other people and genuinely being attentive to them, make it a habit to take note of body language and posture of other people. Training your brain to pay attention to other people and read their emotions instead of only caring about your own feelings promotes empathy and gets your brain to draw attention away from your failures or your perceived shortcomings. For example, while you check in with the people in your support system, take notice of how they're sitting or standing. If they're slouched a little, they're probably feeling pretty comfortable and casual. If they're sitting rigidly, they might be a bit too overly attentive and formal. They also might be uncomfortable or anxious. If they're slouching a lot or are hunched over—and if this isn't normal for the person in question—they might be feeling anxious or stressed out. People who sit rigidly are anxious and want to be attentive so that they can leave if they need to. People who are anxious and slouch over because of their anxiety are making a subconscious show of hiding themselves and making themselves seem small. Taking notes of things like this can promote awareness of others as well as awareness of yourself.

While you watch other people's posture and body language, you should also make a note of your own. The body and mind are often acting together to give you a certain feeling or influence you in a certain way. As an example, you slouch your shoulders and keep your chin down when you're feeling unconfident or if you don't want to be somewhere or feel nervous. You feel this way because your body is that way, and your body is that way because you feel that way—the posture of your body and the feelings you have are connected more often than we might think. Now, if you wanted to feel more confident, it would help you to straighten your back out and look upward. When you position your body this way, you encourage your mind to follow suit. This becomes a feedback loop where you look better to feel better and feel better to look better. When you get in the habit of holding yourself high and holding your body in a way that makes you look confident, you trick your mind into feeling more confident. This is how so many people can seemingly just fake confidence or fake happiness or fake any range of emotions on the spot. When we hold ourselves a certain way and keep our body in mind, we can force ourselves to be more open to that emotion. Keep this in mind when you go through your daily routine. If you feel yourself start to become very anxious or stressed out, clear your throat and straighten your back and jawline. Doing this promotes feelings of calm and confidence. Relax your shoulders, facial muscles, stomach, and any other part of your body where you usually hold your tension. We have a tendency to build up physical stress in our muscles without even meaning to. When we hold this tension in for too long, it has a mental effect on us after a certain frame of time. We want to prevent this buildup of tension at all costs—physical tension can lead to more emotional and mental tension—we need to regularly check in on our bodies and make sure that we aren't overloading ourselves with stress on accident. After you relax your body where you need it most, take a few deep breaths and self-assess. Ask yourself where you are and why you are there. Ask yourself afterward what you are doing and why, and what you want to do next. This is how you can ground yourself better and make sure that your mind isn't being too overloaded with that tension. Chances are if your body is beginning to feel overloaded, your mind is too. So, do what you can to make regular check-ins with yourself and make sure that you aren't feeling too anxious or stressed out at any given point in time. Having these small grounding sessions is also a very good way to distract yourself from whatever was stressing you out and return your mind to a more neutral state where you are relaxed and calm. Grounding yourself is a way that you can deal with not only having a lot of physical and mental stress and anxiety attacks as well as periods of sensory overload, it's also a way that you can back up and assess how you've been doing in the sense of how you're treating others, namely your loved ones or the people around you. When you self-assess, it's a practice in being honest with yourself in a way that isn't self-deprecating or that makes you feel bad about any points you may have had where you lashed out at someone. It's a period of time or healing, where you can be honest to yourself while still being positive and kind to yourself and allowing yourself the space and the time you need to heal and try and nip your issue of overthinking in the bud. When you ground yourself, you also help to keep the paths of communication open so that you can keep being honest and up-front with your support system and they can do the same with you. The failure to properly ground yourself, especially when you're checking in with your loved ones, can make it harder for you to be calm and release some of your tension.

The communication with loved ones and with people who have the medical background to support you are so incredibly important to your healing journey. When you don't try and put your best foot forward in terms of healing and connecting with the people you might be hurting, it makes it seem as though you aren't ready to start healing. Ask yourself before you first sit down with your support system if you are really ready to heal, or if you want to feel better about yourself overnight. This is where you can decide whether you're on the road to getting better, or if you're just having a moment where you feel unconfident and want to feel like a better person—instead turning yourself into the best version of yourself for the betterment of not only you but the people around you and in your support system. You should only face your support system and begin communicating with them about your journey to emotional recovery when you know you can be better and want to get there.

The next chapter will take some of the focus away from the communication with other people and refocus it on the communication with yourself for the purpose of healing. There are so many different ways that different people have been able to recover from a long life of anxiety and overthinking and unhealthy stress, but most of these methods might not work for you. You have to be the one to find out which works best for you so that you can heal not just the fastest, but also in a way that guarantees the new life you lead will be the happiest and most complete version of the life you live now.

CHAPTER 7:

HOLDING YOURSELF ACCOUNTABLE

While it is incredibly important to be able to talk plainly with the people you care about, about your mental health and your emotional journey to recovery from an overactive mind and the stresses that come with it, it's equally, if not more important, to be able to also hold yourself accountable for your actions, your thoughts, and your feelings as you recover.

Understand that there will always be people behind you who will support you throughout your journey, including your friends and family, as well as—hopefully—someone who is specialized and professionally able to help you and advise you on your recovery. However, the people who stand behind you will not move you forward. They can motivate you and give you advice and love and encourage you to take the step forward that you need to if you want to feel better and think healthier, but they cannot take that step for you. You have to be the one to buckle down on your decision and put your best foot forward for the sake of your recovery, both for your own sake and for the sake of others around you. Here are some ways you can best hold yourself accountable throughout the course of your journey, and some things to keep in mind as you do so.

- Make use of your journal—it is meant to serve you throughout your recovery, and it can be used for a multitude of things. Not only can you use it to document your daily feelings and record positive notes that you have so you can motivate yourself, but you can also use it as a way of motivation through self-punishment. You will have bad days, and they need to be documented just as much as the good days. While your best moments should serve to motivate you to continue trying your best to be better and feel better about yourself, your worst moments should serve as examples of how not to act and what to try not to be in the future. Although the way that you "punish" yourself is entirely subjective—you can literally punish yourself if you feel it necessary, or you can just meditate on what went wrong and how to prevent it from happening in the future—there should be some kind of negative stimulus to accompany the bad day or bad thought so that it's less likely to happen going forward. However, you should also remember that you're learning and growing, and you shouldn't harshly punish a small mistake. Understanding that you were wrong and trying to correct yourself is usually all that's ever necessary when you're just starting out on your recovery path. When you have a recurring negative thought or feeling, or you keep making the same mistake over and over again, then it might be time for you to have an intervention with yourself and consider how you can best prevent yourself from doing it again, feeling that way if you can avoid it, or lashing out at other people during or because of it. The goal of you holding yourself accountable is not to punish yourself or make yourself feel bad—the goal is to better yourself and get yourself to succeed in a way that improves your performance emotionally and gets you feeling happier and calmer in your life. So, you shouldn't always go for the harshest punishment when you make a mistake.

- Understand that you are growing and will always continue to grow and that growth is not linear. The way that we develop and change as humans over time is prompted by the changes that we see in the world that we want to adapt to or embody. If we see a wave of positivity moving over society, it's in our brains as humans to want to be more positive in order to fit that mold of society and how society should always be. This development is constant—we have been changing and growing since we were born and we will continue to grow and change as people until we die. Even after we're done growing physically, there's always more to learn and more to experience. Additionally, as we grow older, we see and experience things that might change something in us or prompt us to want to change. The process of change is often long and arduous, and it's harder for some people than it is for others. And, some things are more easily changed than others. Changing a small habit in the way we stand or talk, for example, is much easier than changing the way that we feel and think deep down. So when we do start to try and change the way we feel and think, it's difficult and it can be discouraging when we don't immediately succeed or the change isn't overnight like we might all hope it is. However, most endeavors that take the most time end up being the most rewarding to everyone involved, and they tend to last longer. The longer you commit to something and put time into it consistently, the more of a habit it becomes, and easier it becomes to maintain for a longer period of time. Eventually, these longer habits will last much longer in our lives than any of the shorter habits we might have formed. So, for the sake of keeping up with yourself and making your emotional investments as long-term and successfully so as possible, don't give up on yourself or on your plans! Often, our plans to emotionally transform ourselves start out going really well, and we feel like the entirety of the journey will be a walk in the park. However, after a while, we often begin to dip in progress as we hit a wall. With every wall, we need to change our perspective or consider the way we perceive the problems ahead of us. When we're able to shift our perspective to tackle new problems that face us, we're able to vault ourselves over them quickly and move on with our road to emotional recovery. This is why being open-minded and aware of yourself and of other possibilities is so important when it comes to recovering emotionally. If you hit an emotional wall and begin to lose hope in yourself, it can be hard to try and open your mind to positivity—you feel endlessly negative and as though nothing will ever get better about your situation and emotional state. However, if you can open your mind to the potential for positivity and good things to turn your day around, you're more likely to be successful and get over that emotional hump faster. The most important thing to keep track of while you're recovering is your perspective on that recovery and how fast you can change the way you look at the world. If you can self-assess regularly and understand how to change your perspective without changing your personality or lashing out, you can more easily get over the emotional plateaus that we face so often while we recover from stress, anxiety, and overthinking.

- Adopting spirituality for your own benefit and the benefit of your loved ones can go a long way in helping you to heal both emotionally and mentally. Even adopting a daily ritual of meditation or some light yoga in the morning, or simple mindfulness when you go outside or have breakfast or your morning coffee can evolve the way you act every day and perceive the world for the better. Regardless of your religious affiliation or lack thereof, most people will benefit from trying to heal their souls. It can help them to feel more aligned, more whole as a person, and more fit to help the world and help others. Adopting some kind of spiritual practice and trying to eliminate your bad habits when you can have been shown to help people eliminate stress, anxiety, depression, and many other negative experiences and symptoms which accompany overthinking. When we meditate, we don't just focus on our breathing and on our body—we focus on healing ourselves in every way we can. Meditation and yoga can be a massive help as far as aligning ourselves goes. When we open ourselves up to being connected with the world and the people in it in a way that we might not have been able to do before, we motivate happiness and more contented living in ourselves. Spirituality can also bring us much closer to our friends and families—we feel more connected to ourselves, letting us also be more connected to the people around us.

- Have clear goals that are both short term and long term. While you should always have a long-term goal of what you want to do or how you want to feel by the time you've more or less healed yourself, it's also very important to set goals that you can regularly check in on and update as you move forward. For example, you may have a long-term goal of stopping yourself from being so anxious—this is a good goal to have, but it can take a while to see results in that endeavor. We keep short-term goals as well as long-term goals because with short-term goals, we can see results faster and feel more satisfied with our progress, so we feel the necessary encouragement to keep going. So, instead of having only that long-term goal, it might be a good idea to set a smaller goal, like "do three nice things today", or paying ten people compliments in a week.

Things like this are not only faster and yield results quicker, but they also provide a sense of schedule that you might not feel with longer goals. With these shorter, more regular goals, we have the ability to actively monitor our progress throughout the weeks, months, and years. When we can keep a steady pace, even if that pace includes small deeds, it's encouraging and it motivates us to keep pushing forward. Think of it as an exercise routine—although it might be a bit of a long time in order for you to see the results that you had in mind when you began the program or regimen, you can notice smaller changes faster than the overall shift towards better health. The same can be said for mental health—even if you don't immediately become the person that you want to be by the "end" of your healing journey, there are smaller, less noticeable changes that can prove to you that you are improving, even if it might not always feel like it. Even if you aren't the perfect person right now, and you still have bad days where it's incredibly difficult to control your thoughts and emotions, just stop every now and then and take note of the way you view the world. Chances are, you've already had something of a positive shift in your life that should serve to just motivate you even more.

- There's an important difference between motivation and discipline. When we set out to complete a job, we feel that short-lived but intense burst of energy we usually feel when we're excited to start something new. We're fascinated with the process and, even though we might not know yet how it will turn out, we're excited at the moment to find out. When we begin the journey, it feels great. We're making fast progress and it feels like we're getting better every single day. When we make these fast changes to our life, we have a short burst of time where we feel incredibly motivated to make those changes and stick to them. At that moment, we feel like we're on top of the world and we feel unstoppable. But, that short-lived feeling of being invincible is usually pretty short and ends abruptly. We hit the plateau after we have that massive spark of energy, and it can feel discouraging when we hit that bump in the road. When we plateau, we've just hit our first landmark in the journey to bettering ourselves, where we have to implement changes and struggle to uphold them. This can be stressful if we aren't used to doing this. If we aren't used to having to change our perspective and combat obstacles in our path, we might feel as though this change wasn't meant for us to begin with. However, this couldn't be further from the truth. When you plateau and start having to struggle to make any progress at all, take it as a sign that you're headed in the right direction, and that you need to keep pushing. The motivation we feel when we start out is easy to disrupt, and it doesn't tend to last very long. This motivation when we begin is often unreliable, and you shouldn't use it as a reason to get out of bed. The entire point of making a change in your life is to make your own decisions and stick to them even when you don't feel like it, or when you're tired. Instead, you have to learn to discipline yourself to feel good and to act on the beginnings of your motivation. If you can do that, you can start getting over obstacles faster because you have the determination and the willpower to force yourself to stand by your beliefs and keep those changes in your life going. While motivation tends to feel better, and it sometimes makes us more energetic when it comes to making these changes, it ultimately lies with the power of our own sheer will to make sure those changes remain throughout the course of our journey. The determination and the discipline of the self doesn't feel as good or as liberating at first as the whim of motivation, but it will always be so much more rewarding when you look back at how far you've come.

- You are never gone growing, and you should never think of yourself as being done growing. When we begin a spiritual journey, it never ends. When we set out to make changes to ourselves, our bodies, or our minds, in any facet, our work is never truly done in that endeavor. The more work we put into it, the more benefits we will reap of it. So, we should always strive to be better than we were yesterday. To be more physical, think about an exercise regimen you might have started. After a while, you see the results you have been hoping to see for so long—you finally feel content with how you look and feel. However, you have to maintain those habits to keep feeling your best. So, even when you've completed your long-term goal, there's still a lot you can always be doing as far as self-improvement and holding yourself accountable for your own life choices and the improvements you make to yourself. If you decide to make a change to your lifestyle, you have to be willing to keep at it and keep yourself not only motivated but disciplined. Even when you've reached all your goals and you feel that you've peaked, you now have the responsibility to yourself and the people in your support system to keep up with those positive habits and keep making yourself reinforce them day after day. When you get into this habit or keeping up with yourself, you can genuinely revolutionize the way that you perceive the world and the way that you perceive yourself. The more you keep pace with your own improvement, and keep finding ways to improve yourself even after you feel you've peaked, the more you'll just keep improving and feeling and thinking better.

The most important message that you should keep in mind while you go about your journey of self-improvement and decreasing your anxiety is that you are in control of everything you do, and there are people around you who will always support you.

You are the most important part of your recovery. No matter what you do, how fast you begin to accelerate, how fast you plateau, and how fast you're able to change your perspective and tackle the obstacles in front of you, you have to be the one to put one foot in front of the other and make yourself get out of bed every morning in order to keep going, keep improving, and keep making yourself think and feel better. The point of self-improvement is never to prove a point to other people—it's only ever to feel better about yourself and have a better relationship with not only yourself but the rest of the world and the other people in it.

That being said, the people in your support group should never be taken for granted. The more you rely on the people in your support system, the more you should also find a way to take steps on your own toward becoming better and being more independent. It's good to both be independent from the people in your life, and open to help from them when you need it. They're people in your life who are more than ready to help you at any given point in time, and you need to be able to accept that help if you want to see the fastest progress.

The next chapter will finish out with some notes about the

self and how we can manage it in a way that relieves some of the daily stresses off our shoulders. While it's important to make sure we can handle whatever life throws at us, it's also important to be sure we know when to cut our losses and understand when it just isn't emotionally healthy for us to be involved in something. Being emotionally aware is one of the most important things about being mentally and physically aware.

CHAPTER 8:

KEEP IT UP

It's so incredibly important to not only be comfortable with yourself as it pertains to healing yourself and the people around you while you go through that journey but to be able to actively make your life happier as you go through it. Often, you develop a lot of anxiety as a result of negative emotions or simply a lack of emotion. The apathy we feel is a direct derivative of anxiety, and we overthink because our brain doesn't have any emotions to focus on, so it creates its own out of anxiety, stress, and apathy. When we make up these negative emotions, there are no positive emotions we've made up to counteract them—when we naturally feel a positive or negative emotion brought on by something entirely outside our own perception. There tends to be a negative or positive emotion brought on afterward, which tends to counteract that first emotion. This way, we're emotionally balanced and we have less hitches in the emotional road. When we don't experience these emotions because of something that happens to us, and we just make them up because we don't experience the world enough to be able to have those experiences which are independent of our experiences as a human being.

The most relevant part of healing is having those positive emotions brought back so that you give yourself positive experiences without the need to stress yourself out unnecessarily. For example, going outside and disconnecting from your devices for a little while can go a long way in stimulating positive emotions. We feel good when we go outside and smell the fresh air, and we feel good when we feel the most connected to the ground beneath us. Because being outside stimulates this kind of very basic pleasure in us, you should seek it out when you can. This doesn't have to be a part of your regimen, which you keep up with daily, but you should go outside fairly often so that you can really experience the real world around you for what it is in a basic, carnal way. Going outside doesn't have to be a solitary experience, either. It can be relaxing and cathartic to just take a walk outside with friends or other loved ones. It helps you not only to calm down, but it can be a good way for you to talk plainly with the people you care about and who care about you. Letting them into your life in a more honest and up-front way is a good venue for you to be happier in the long run. Being in nature tends to have this effect on people—we feel calmer and more emotionally stable and relaxed when we're outside, so it makes sense that we might be more willing to reach out to people and talk with them honestly about their lives, how they feel, as well as our own experiences with them. Having these experiences mesh together over a length of time can be incredibly healing for everyone involved.

When you feel overwhelmed with the pressures of life, and you feel as though you might collapse under the weight of your own stresses, it's a good time to step back and have an in-depth look at why you are where you are and why you're doing what you're doing. Assess yourself and your position in the moment and determine how important that position is to you. Your mental and emotional health should always come before the wants of others and what they might demand from you. If there's someone in your life who's asking something of you and it would just be too much, you have the ability and the freedom to decline in an exercise of putting yourself first.

Often, a lot of your stress arises from not knowing how to prioritize yourself above other people. When we learn this irreplaceable skill, we become aware of our place with our friends and loved ones and we understand better how we can make ourselves and our lives happier. If you're in a place or position where you don't feel happy, get out of that situation. You aren't being terrible or selfish for wanting the best for yourself and wanting to be happy for the sake of being happy. Even if you don't want people to view you as selfish, there are more important things in your life than pleasing others instead of pleasing yourself. Be hedonistic on an intimate, spiritual level. There are ways that you can please yourself on the level of the emotions and the brain which you might not have been able to do or work up the courage to commit to before you started trying to undo all the trauma done to you over time. Indulge in something you enjoy now and then, splurge on something you've had your eye on for a while, turn down plans if you don't feel like going out, and have days to yourself where you can just sit back, relax, and enjoy your own company in a way that you might not be able to if there was anyone else around, no matter how close to you they were. When we prioritize ourselves and learn to simply cut our losses emotionally, we free ourselves to so many healing experiences we would never have had if we didn't know how to make those changes and make decisions for the sake of our mental health instead of for the sake of the happiness of other people. Even so much as taking a day off from your obligations if you can, and having just an afternoon where you can indulge and treat yourself can be an incredibly healing experience in and of itself. Indulging yourself and accepting yourself as someone who needs to be cared for and loved, even if it has to be by you, can bring you so much joy and emotional release that you might never have had access to otherwise.

Ultimately, there might be people in your life who are preventing you from being this best version of yourself. These people are toxic people, and they might be involved in any part of your life. They might be your friends, your family, your coworkers, or anyone else in your support system, or out of it, who you talk to regularly and who are having a direct negative impact on your life. Toxic people can look any range of ways, and they come in many disguises. You might have been a toxic person at one point—most people have toxic traits or traits in their personality which could be improved to make them more pleasant to be around and healthy for themselves and for others. Regardless of whether or not you have toxic traits now or did before, that doesn't mean you can't be affected by them in other people today. The more you learn about people in your life, the more easily you might begin to see them for what they truly are. If you know a toxic person in your life, you'll likely know by the way they act before the way they look. Toxic people tend to manipulate others in order to get what they want, and they don't tend to feel a lot of remorse when they successfully manipulate other people into doing what they need them to do. Toxic people get other, submissive people to do their dirty work for them while they sit back and manipulate everyone else behind the scenes. Toxic people might have very depressive actions, they might be anxious, they might be narcissistic, they could have any number of symptoms of other mental illnesses or signs that they aren't all there or they have plans and abilities to manipulate you to get what they want and think they deserve. You have probably been manipulated by a toxic person at some point in the last month or two. You also probably have at least one person in your life who would be considered toxic. Consider if someone you know or someone even in your support system has ever used the powers of eloquence and their own words against you to blackmail you or guilt you into being in emotional debt to them. Do they hold grudges against you for things that happened ages ago and might not have even been your fault? Do they have any way of guilting you or gaslighting you by playing the victim until you give in to their rhetoric and do what they want? If this is the case, you're dealing with a toxic manipulator and you can free up your life and your soul if you drop them as quickly as you can. Once you eliminate them from your life, you can feel yourself healing from all the bad energy that was with you with that person. Don't think of it as a major loss if you lose them for good—manipulators tend to be dramatic and make large shows out of abandoning people and making them feel pretty difficult. When we do knock them down, they might try to re-enter or take advantage of other people or things in our lives so we don't force them out. This can be incredibly disturbing, so always have a way you can protect yourself and other people from people like this who are potentially dangerous or obsessive. The point of cutting off dangerous or otherwise very toxic people is not to put you in danger or even to stand up for what is right. You should want to cut off people who make you sad and angry—people who make your life less enjoyable to live every day and people you have lost your precious time to for having to take care of them and cater to them. You drop toxic people for no one else's sake but your own, no matter what.

That is the nature of toxic people and removing them from your life. When you initially take them out, it feels as though something is gone, wrong, or missing. However, as time goes on and the hole begins to close, we often realize the hole should never have existed in the first place. Something new and better and healthy might have even begun to sprout in its place. If this is the case, be sure to foster whatever is growing anew. It might be something healthy that will enrich your experience and help you to be happier overall. It might be something toxic that is growing in that place of its toxic parent, in which case you can nip toxic behavior in the bud before it gets too bad.

When we overthink, it feels as though it controls our lives. Every move we make and every thought we have feels as though it's already been governed by this force in our head, which tells us that no matter what, we'll fail. No matter what we'll feel worthless, we'll never succeed no matter what, and so on and so forth. This impact can be damaging, not only to our professional career but also to our intimate, personal lives. The way being constantly told we don't meet some kind of invisible standard and never will as a kid messes with you in a way that is incomparable to many other experiences you can have while growing up. However, while you grow up, reflect on who got you there. You are always growing up, no matter how old you are, so always assess yourself and reflect on how you did today and how you did tomorrow. When you're constantly self-assessing in a way that is constructive, you can get so much done and quickly become the best version of yourself. Being aware of yourself, your emotions, and your mind is the best way that you can stay on track and make sure you become the best person you can be.

CONCLUSION

Thank you for making it through to the end of *Overthinking*, let's hope it was informative and able to provide you with all of the tools you need to achieve your goals whatever they may be.

The next step is to take the first real steps toward recovery and get on your way to being a kinder, more wholesome person with less stress in your body and mind.

Finally, if you found this book useful in any way, a review on Amazon is always appreciated!

Printed in Great Britain
by Amazon